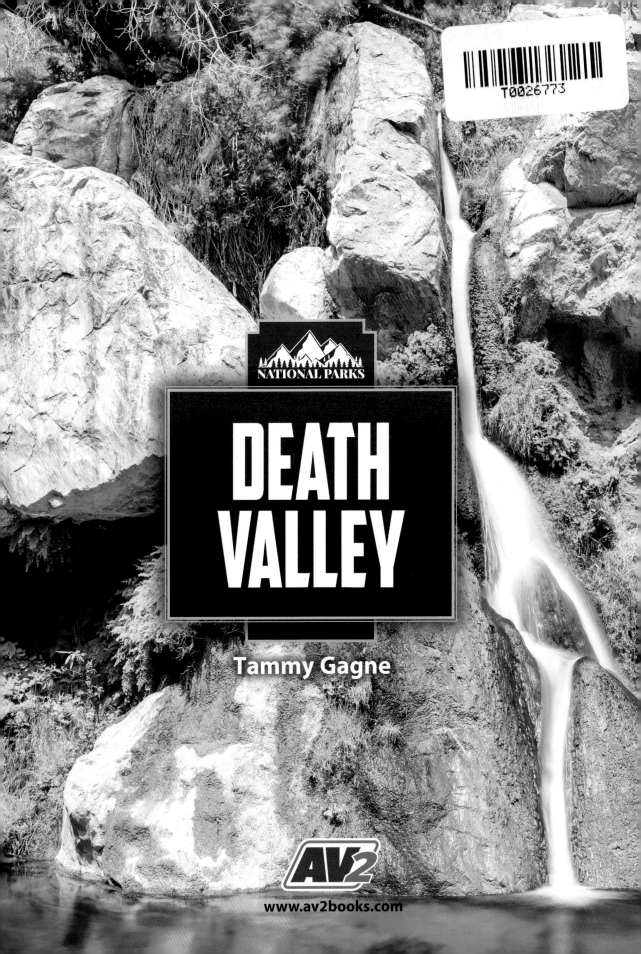

NATIONAL PARKS

DEATH VALLEY

Tammy Gagne

AV2

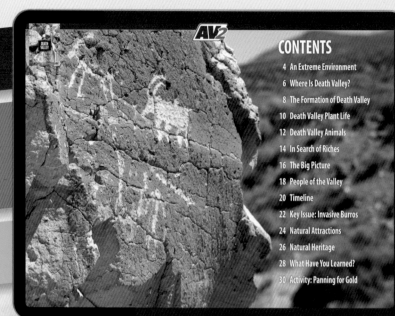

CONTENTS

AV2 is optimized for use on any device

Your interactive eBook comes with...

Contents
Browse a live contents page to easily navigate through resources

Audio
Listen to sections of the book read aloud

Videos
Watch informative video clips

Weblinks
Gain additional information for research

Try This!
Complete activities and hands-on experiments

Key Words
Study vocabulary, and complete a matching word activity

Quizzes
Test your knowledge

Slideshows
View images and captions

... and much, much more!

DEATH VALLEY

CONTENTS

An Extreme Environment

Death Valley National Park is one of the most dangerous places on Earth. This desert region is both the hottest and the driest area in all of North America. There is still much to see, however. The landscape holds everything from mountains to valleys, and sand dunes to **salt pans**.

Although it is surrounded by mountain ranges, the park is home to the lowest point of elevation on the entire continent. The valley itself stretches north–south for about 140 miles (225 kilometers). Almost all of it—550 square miles (1,425 square km)—lies below sea level.

Death Valley is the **largest** U.S. national park south of Alaska. It covers an area of **3.4 million** acres (1.4 million hectares).

The Death Valley region gets an average of **2.4 inches** (6.1 centimeters) of rain each year.

Scientists have recorded temperatures as high as **134 degrees Fahrenheit** (57° Celsius) in parts of Death Valley.

Even though Death Valley is known for its desert environment, the park does have at least one waterfall. Darwin Falls is located in the Panamint Valley. It is fed by underground springs.

More than 1 million tourists flock to the park each year to experience its extreme environment and its breathtaking views. However, at one time, there were no hotels or tour guides to assist travelers. In the past, people journeying through the region risked their lives to make it to the other side.

A key draw for Death Valley visitors is Scotty's Castle. The Spanish-style mansion was built in the 1920s as a vacation home for a Chicago businessman.

MAPPING DEATH VALLEY

NEVADA

CALIFORNIA

• Sacramento

• San Francisco

Pacific Ocean

• Los Angeles

San Diego •

LEGEND

N

- California
- Death Valley
- Nevada
- Mexico
- • City
- Water

MAP SCALE 0 |———————| 100 Miles
                    100 Km

Where Is Death Valley?

Death Valley National Park is located at the north end of the Mojave Desert. The park is almost entirely in the southwestern part of California. A small section lies in the neighboring state of Nevada. The Nevada state line forms much of the park's northeastern border. The Inyo Mountains and Inyo Forest lie to the west of the park. To the southeast are the Greenwater Mountains. The Slate Range borders the park on the southwest.

California and Nevada are both known for their hot, arid climates. The extreme temperatures of Death Valley are the result of the valley's shape, depth, surrounding terrain, and weather. The Sun shines over the valley almost every day. This continual sunlight heats up both the air and the ground. However, when the heat radiates off the rocks and soil, it cannot move far. This is because it becomes trapped by the surrounding mountains. The heat stays within the valley as a result.

The Mojave Desert is considered to be the smallest desert in the United States. It covers an area of approximately 25,000 square miles (64,750 sq. km).

PUZZLER

Deserts are places that get very little rain or snow. They are not always in hot places, however. The United States is home to both hot and cold deserts.

Q: Which of the deserts below are hot? Which are cold?

CANADA

Great Basin Desert

A

Mojave Desert

B

Sonoran Desert

C

Chihuahuan Desert

D

Pacific Ocean

Gulf of Mexico

MEXICO

ANSWERS: A. Cold B. Hot C. Hot D. Hot

The Formation of Death Valley

During the **Paleozoic Era**, the region now called Death Valley lay underneath a large, shallow sea. **Geologists** have learned this by studying ancient limestone and sandstone found at the edges of the valley. Shifting plates within Earth's crust caused the ground to rise up. This movement pushed the water farther westward over time.

The exposed land went through additional changes during the **Mesozoic Era**. Although several mountain ranges in what is now southeastern California and Nevada formed during this period, other land masses underwent intense **erosion**. Some mountains became hills. Some hills became valleys.

About 3 million years ago, the movements in the crust changed. Instead of pushing together, the plates began pulling apart. This movement created more mountains and valleys, including Death Valley.

With an elevation of 282 feet (86 meters) below sea level, Badwater Basin is the lowest point in North America. As low as it is, movement in Earth's crust slowly continues to dip its floor farther below sea level.

FROM SEA TO SALT PAN

Long after the shallow sea moved westward, water once again filled Death Valley. This happened about 50,000 years ago, during Earth's last **Ice Age**. At this time, the Death Valley region was one of many lakes in the area. In some places, the water was about 600 feet (183 m) deep. As the Ice Age ended, this water disappeared through **evaporation**.

Salt Creek is one of the last remnants of the freshwater lake that once covered Death Valley. The water became salt-based as the lake dried up.

The last time Death Valley held a substantial amount of water was about 3,000 years ago. This shallow lake also evaporated. When it did, large amounts of salt were left behind. This created the salt pan that still exists in the valley today. The salt pan in Badwater Basin covers about 200 square miles (518 sq. km).

The salt flat at Badwater Basin is made up of a series of salt polygons. These multi-sided shapes are created when the mud underneath the flat dries and cracks.

Death Valley Plant Life

With so little **precipitation**, it is difficult to imagine plants surviving in Death Valley. However, more than 1,000 different **species** thrive in the valley and surrounding areas. Which plants grow where depends largely on elevation.

The higher areas receive more rainfall than the desert floor. This allows more plants to grow there. Spiny blackbrush, with their yellow flowers, bloom from April to June. Trees such as bristlecone pines, limber pines, and Joshua trees also grow there. At lower elevations, visitors can see creosote bushes, desert holly, and mesquite. Pickleweed and saltgrass can be found in the marshes and springs that line the salt pan. The salt pan itself only grows vegetation at the **microscopic** level.

Death Valley's plants have had to adapt to find and retain the water they need to survive. Some plants grow long roots that soak up water from deep in the ground. Other plants have shorter root systems that extend over a wide horizontal range. They get their water from short-lived ponds that form after it rains. Cacti have developed thick skins that slow evaporation. This allows them to use water over a long period.

Honey mesquite trees survive well in the dry climate of Death Valley. Their roots can extend more than 100 feet (30 m) into the ground to reach water.

SUPER BLOOM

Every few years, Death Valley's dry, barren desert floor becomes a kaleidoscope of color. Millions of wildflowers blanket the ground in a collective bloom, bringing the valley to life. This rare event has come to be known as a "super bloom."

Certain conditions have to be met for a super bloom to occur. Rainfall plays a key role. A super bloom requires heavy rain in early autumn, followed by regular rain throughout the winter months. The weather must also remain warm throughout these months, and the winds low.

Beneath the ground are great numbers of plant seeds. Some have come from the few plants that grow in the valley. Others have blown into the valley from other places. Most of these seeds have sat in the ground for years because there was not enough water for them to grow. When the rains arrive and the other conditions are met, all of these seeds come to life at once, forming a super bloom.

Death Valley's most recent super bloom took place in 2016. This was more than 10 years after the next most recent bloom, which occurred in 2005.

Death Valley Animals

Although most humans find Death Valley's environment too harsh to call home, many animal species can be found living in the region. Most of them have adapted over time to require less drinking water than other animals. Bighorn sheep can go several days without drinking during hot weather. When they do find water, they can drink up to 2 gallons (7.6 liters). This helps them survive the drier periods. Kangaroo rats can actually live their entire lives without ever drinking a single drop of water. They have special kidneys that make this possible.

Water is not the only challenge of living in Death Valley. Animals must also deal with the raging heat. Some of them simply avoid it. The desert turtle hides underground in a burrow for months at a time during the hottest parts of the year. Other animals hunt for food at night when temperatures are slightly lower. After resting all day, coyotes roam Death Valley's sand dunes each evening, chasing the jackrabbits that also inhabit the region.

The long-nosed leopard lizard is one of Death Valley's many reptile species. It can be found throughout the region, in areas ranging from the valley floor to elevations of 3,600 feet (1,097 m).

NIGHT VISITORS

People camping in Death Valley have been known to have visitors at night. Attracted by the campfires, kit foxes sometimes drop in at campsites. While kit foxes are considered to be friendly and curious, they are just as wild as the other animals in the area. They spend their nights hunting a wide variety of mammals, reptiles, and fish.

Like most desert animals, the kit fox has features that help it live in this extreme environment. Its big ears are useful for regulating heat. The ears are packed with blood vessels. These vessels radiate heat from the fox's body, helping it to stay cool. A kit fox's feet also help the animal survive the heat. Its paws are covered with fur, even on the foot pads and between the toes. This fur protects the kit fox's feet when it has to walk on the scorching ground.

There has been growing concern for Death Valley's kit fox population in recent years. The kit fox competes with other animals for habitat and food. Its main competitor is the coyote. The number of coyotes living in Death Valley is on the rise. This has put the future of the kit fox more at risk.

Although it is part of the dog family, the kit fox is no bigger than a housecat.

In Search of Riches

In 1848, gold was discovered in California. This discovery launched what is now known as the California Gold Rush. Tens of thousands of people journeyed west in the hope of striking it rich.

Most people traveled on established trails. However, some thought that the trip would take less time if they went through the desert. It is estimated that about 100 wagons of gold-seekers took this route. Faced with the grueling heat and the rocky terrain, many people turned back. Others became lost and spent weeks searching for a way out. When these people finally reached the other side, they named the area Death Valley.

Other people soon began exploring the valley. It was not long before they found that it had valuable resources of its own. Silver, gold, and **borax** were mined in the valley into the early 1900s. When mining operations began to slow, one of the mining companies turned its buildings into a resort. Death Valley slowly became a tourist destination. To ensure that the valley's natural environment was preserved, President Herbert Hoover named it a national monument in 1933. It would be another 61 years before Death Valley became a national park.

The Wildrose Charcoal Kilns are a reminder of the park's mining past. The beehive-shaped kilns provided fuel for mining operations by converting wood to charcoal.

BIOGRAPHY

Franklin Delano Roosevelt (1882–1945)

While Herbert Hoover was the first person to officially recognize the importance of Death Valley, it was another president that began shaping the land for public use. Franklin Delano Roosevelt came to office only a few weeks after Death Valley was named a national monument. The country was in the middle of the **Great Depression** at the time, and many people were out of work.

To get people working again, Roosevelt created the Civilian Conservation Corps (CCC). Made up of unemployed men, the CCC was responsible for making upgrades to national lands. Work at Death Valley began in the fall of 1933 and continued for nine years. Roads and scenic trails were built, as well as picnic grounds and camping areas. Water and telephone lines were also set up. Under Roosevelt, Death Valley became a place that people could enjoy instead of endure.

Roosevelt remained president until 1945. He led the country through both the Great Depression and World War II. He died while still in office, at the age of 63.

FACTS OF LIFE

Born: January 30, 1882

Hometown: Hyde Park, New York

Occupation: Politician

Died: April 12, 1945

Deserts exist on every continent of the world. These **biomes** are the driest areas on the planet. Most receive fewer than 10 inches (25 cm) of rain each year. Inner regions of Antarctica, the world's largest cold desert, get less than 2 inches (5 cm) of snow each year.

North America

Atlantic Ocean

Pacific Ocean

South America

Mojave Desert
United States

Atacama Desert
Chile

Southern Ocean

LEGEND

- Water
- Land
- Antarctica

N

MAP SCALE

0 — 2,000 Miles
2,000 Km

Tabernas Desert
Spain

Gobi Desert
Mongolia and China

Europe

Asia

Africa

Pacific Ocean

Indian Ocean

Australia

Kalahari Desert
Botswana, Namibia, and South Africa

Great Sandy Desert
Australia

Antarctica

People of the Valley

The Timbisha Shoshone were living in and around Death Valley long before the California Gold Rush. Unlike the gold-seekers, they found that the area met all of their needs. The men hunted desert animals with bows and arrows. The women collected pinyon pine nuts and mesquite beans in baskets that they made themselves.

The Gold Rush forever changed life for the Timbisha Shoshone. It brought newcomers to the area. These people took over much of the land the Timbisha Shoshone called home. In 1866, Congress signed an agreement with the Timbisha Shoshone. The agreement gave the United States the right to travel through the region. It also stated that the land still belonged to the Timbisha Shoshone.

Within a century, however, the United States had taken the land as its own. In 1936, the National Park Service (NPS) set aside 40 acres (16 ha) of land in the Death Valley region for the Timbisha Shoshone. Today, only a few dozen Timbisha Shoshone remain in the area.

When the U.S. government signed the agreement with the Timbisha Shoshone, the country was embroiled in the Civil War. The agreement ensured that the government would be able to access the gold it needed to finance the war.

PUZZLER

The Timbisha Shoshone lived entirely off the land. They made their food, clothing, and tools from items found in nature.

Q. What materials do you think the Timbisha Shoshone women used to make their baskets?

ANSWER: Timbisha Shoshone women used plants that grew in the region for making baskets. These included sumac, willow, and yucca.

TIMELINE

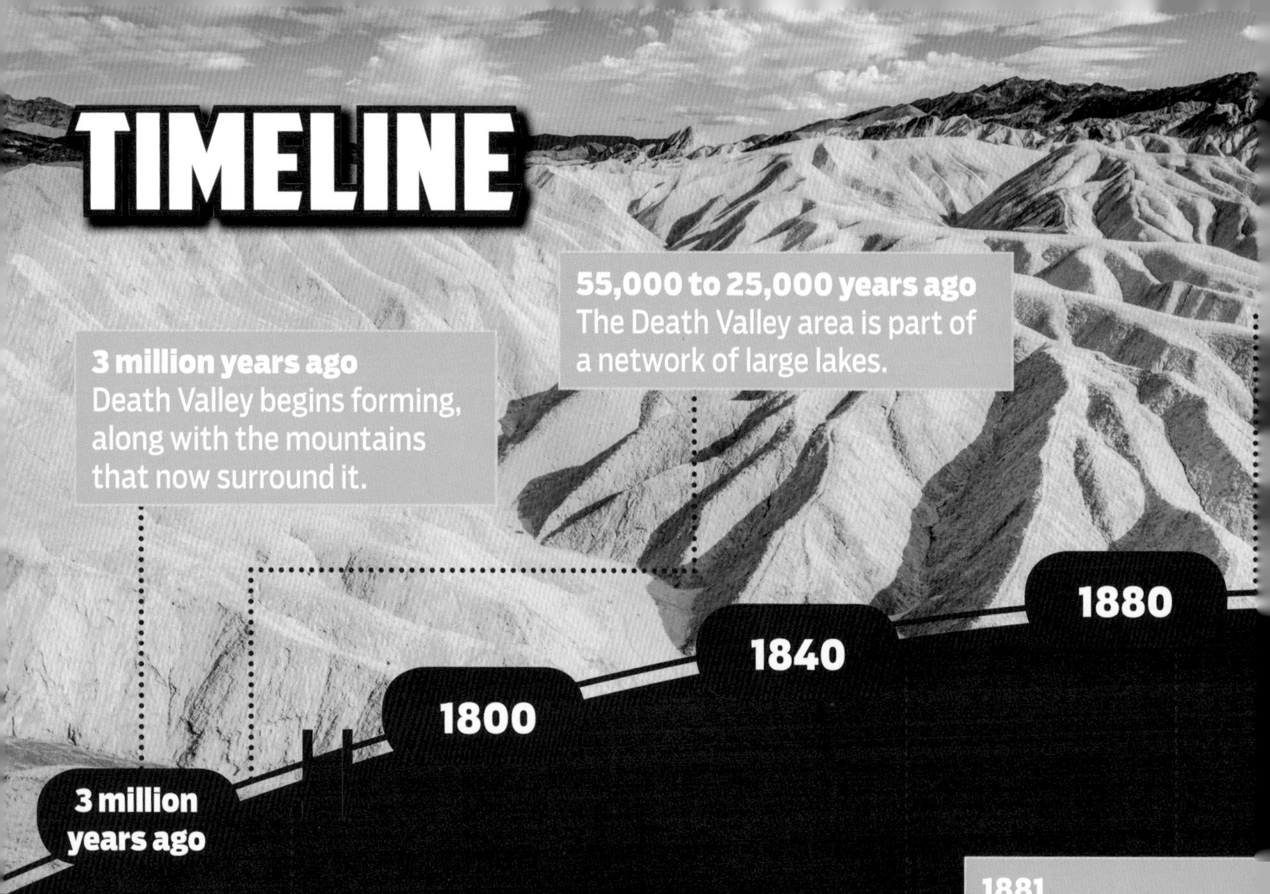

3 million years ago
Death Valley begins forming, along with the mountains that now surround it.

55,000 to 25,000 years ago
The Death Valley area is part of a network of large lakes.

1880

1840

1800

3 million years ago

10,000 years ago
The lakes dry up. They leave behind the exposed valley.

1881
Aaron and Rosie Winters discover borax deposits in Death Valley. Mining operations soon come to the region.

1848
John Wilson Marshall finds flakes of gold in the American River near what is now Sacramento, California. Thousands of **prospectors** soon follow.

1891
An act of Congress launches the Death Valley Expedition. Its purpose is to study the animals and plants in the region.

1994
Congress names Death Valley a national park. The government also expands its size to 3.3 million acres (1.3 million ha).

1930

1960

1990

2020

1933
The CCC begins developing the Death Valley region. The workers construct roads, buildings, and an airplane landing field.

2019
President Donald Trump signs a land transfer agreement that sees Death Valley National Park increase in size by 35,000 acres (14,164 ha).

2018
Death Valley has its hottest month on record, with the temperature averaging 108.1°F (42.3°C) in August.

KEY ISSUE

INVASIVE BURROS

When humans introduce new species to a region, those animals or plants affect the ones that already inhabit the area. Over time, several new species have been brought into Death Valley National Park. Each of these **invasive** species has impacted the region in one way or another. However, the most contested of these species is the burro, or donkey.

Burros were brought to Death Valley by early prospectors. The animals were used to carry tools and belongings from one site to another. When they were no longer needed, the burros were set free to live in the valley. Over time, their population has expanded. Today, as many as 4,000 burros roam free in Death Valley.

An average burro weighs between 400 and 500 pounds (181 and 227 kilograms).

Should Death Valley's burro population be allowed to stay in the park?

Yes	No
The Death Valley burros represent an important time in American history.	There are many historic sites in the park that showcase the valley's past. These burros are only distant relatives of the original burros.
The burros have lived in the park for so long that it should now be considered their home.	The burros are impacting not only native animals, but native plants as well. Many plants are at risk of disappearing due to the burros' large appetite.
Burros are a protected species under the Wild Free-Roaming Horses and Burros Act of 1971.	National parks are exempt from the Act and do not have to treat burros as a protected animal. They can be removed and even destroyed if necessary.

Burros eat large amounts of grasses, shrubs, and other plants. This makes it more difficult for animals native to the valley to find food. The valley's bighorn sheep have been most affected by the growing burro population.

Many people think the burros should be removed from Death Valley. Others disagree. Still, efforts are being made to at least reduce the number of burros in the park. In 2018, the NPS signed an agreement that would see 2,500 burros captured and sent to sanctuaries in other

Natural Attractions

Most tourists make the Furnace Creek Visitor Center their first stop when visiting Death Valley National Park. Its staff can offer detailed information about which attractions are the best for a particular time of year. Furnace Creek is also where visitors will find hotels, campgrounds, and restaurants.

Hikers often head to Golden Canyon to take in its splendid views. There are a variety of trails into the canyon, ranging from short walks to more challenging climbs. Hikers can even combine the trails for a fuller experience. The time of year makes a big difference in where and how long a visitor to Death Valley should hike, however. The park advises against summer hiking in the lowest elevations.

Visitors interested in Death Valley's volcanic history can take a trip to Ubehebe Crater. The crater is what is left of an old maar volcano. This type of volcano is created when **magma** comes into contact with water on Earth's surface. The Ubehebe Crater is about 0.5 miles (0.8 km) wide and 600 feet (183 m) deep. People can stand at the top and look inside or take a hiking trail to the bottom.

Golden Canyon is one of Death Valley's most popular hiking spots. Hikers marvel at its many colorful rock formations.

BE PREPARED

Before venturing outdoors in Death Valley National Park, it is important that visitors are fully prepared for the extreme conditions. Exposure to both the sunlight and heat can cause health problems if people do not take steps to protect themselves.

Bring Water It is important that people stay hydrated in the extreme heat. This makes water a necessity when visiting Death Valley. Visitors should drink at least 0.5 to 1 gallon (2 to 4 L) of water each day.

Cover Up Visitors to Death Valley are at high risk of sunburn and **heatstroke**. To ensure limited exposure to the intense sun, all visitors should cover up with sunglasses, sunblock, and a hat.

Stay Light Experts recommend that people wear light colors when visiting the park. Sunlight tends to reflect off light colors more than dark. This means that light colors do not absorb as much heat.

Tread Carefully Death Valley has a varied terrain. While some parts are easy to traverse, others are more challenging. Having sturdy footwear with good treads, such as hiking boots or athletic shoes, will help visitors stay on track.

Natural Heritage

The Timbisha Shoshone have always had a strong connection to Death Valley. It provided them with food and a place to live. However, the land met more than just survival needs. It also held deep spiritual significance. Symbols of Timbisha Shoshone spirituality can be found in many parts of the park.

One of the key symbols of the Timbisha Shoshone culture are rock carvings called petroglyphs. They are found etched onto rock faces in remote canyons. The carvings often reflect life in the past. Other parts of the park hold a different type of rock formation. Stones placed in a circle were used during a **vision quest**. The circle created a place for a person to stay while waiting for a vision to come and provide guidance.

Most of the areas containing these landmarks remain closed to public view. This is to show respect for the Timbisha Shoshone and their beliefs. People who encounter them are asked not to touch or move any of the objects. This preserves them for future generations.

Death Valley's petroglyphs serve as reminders of what life was like in the past for the Timbisha Shoshone. Some feature animals that were important to their survival, such as bighorn sheep.

THE QUEEN OF DEATH VALLEY

Timbisha Shoshone mythology refers to a time when Death Valley was covered by grassy meadows and trees. This lush environment included a large lake and many streams. Numerous game animals roamed the area. The Timbisha Shoshone grew bountiful crops of corn, beans, and squash in the rich soil.

Life was good for the Timbisha Shoshone. The only problem was the queen who ruled over them. She forced her people to start building her a magnificent stone mansion. She even turned her own family members into slaves for this project. Many years later, it still was not finished. The queen was furious, and her fit of rage led to the death of her own daughter. Before the young girl died, however, she put a curse on her mother's kingdom.

The Timbisha Shoshone say that this curse caused the land to turn on the queen. All the lush vegetation died. The lake and springs dried up. The animals fled. Finally, the people left as well. The queen was left to die in this harsh new region. She met her end alone because of her own greed.

Corn, beans, and squash are often referred to as "The Three Sisters." These three crops were central to the lives of many Native American groups, supplying them with many of the nutrients they needed to survive.

WHAT HAVE YOU LEARNED?

TRUE OR FALSE?

Decide whether the following statements are true or false. If the statement is false, make it true.

1 Most of Death Valley National Park is located in the U.S. state of Nevada.

2 Death Valley is the largest national park in the United States.

3 Bighorn sheep can live their entire lives without drinking any water.

4 Death Valley was named by gold-seekers traveling through the region.

5 In 1956, the NPS set aside 40 acres (16 ha) of land for the Timbisha Shoshone.

6 Death Valley's burros are considered an invasive species.

ANSWERS
1. False. Most of the park is located in California.
2. False. It is the largest national park south of Alaska.
3. False. Kangaroo rats can do this.
4. True.
5. False. This happened in 1936.
6. True.

SHORT ANSWER

Answer the following questions using information from the book.

1 In which desert is Death Valley located?

2 Which part of Death Valley is home to the salt pan?

3 How many plant species are found in Death Valley?

4 Who created the CCC?

5 How much water should visitors to the area drink?

MULTIPLE CHOICE

Choose the best answer for the following questions.

1 How many visitors does Death Valley National Park receive each year?

   a. About 10,000
   b. About 100,000
   c. More than 1 million

2 When did Earth's plates in Death Valley start pulling apart?

   a. 250 million years ago
   b. 3 million years ago
   c. 11,700 years ago

3 What types of plants grow in Death Valley's salt pan?

   a. Microscopic vegetation only
   b. Bristlecone pine trees
   c. Desert holly and mesquite

4 When did Congress pass the Wild Free-Roaming Horses and Burros Act?

   a. 1933
   b. 1971
   c. 1994

PANNING FOR GOLD

Today, large machines are used to mine for gold. In the 1800s, however, prospectors panned for gold. This process allows a person to separate gold from sand and gravel using a shallow pan. See if you can find gold by panning in a stream near your home.

Materials

Small scoop or sand shovel

A shallow pan

Instructions

1. With an adult's help, find a spot in the stream where the water's current is slow-moving. Stand at the water's edge, and use the scoop to dig gravel and sand from the bottom of the stream. Put the gravel and sand into your pan. Try to get the pan 3/4 full.

2. Gently remove larger pieces of rock from the pan to make it easier to inspect its contents.

3. Dip the pan into the water, just under the surface. Shake the pan slowly in a side-to-side motion. This movement will allow the lighter-weight items to float to the pan's surface.

4. Remove dirt, moss, and other debris from the pan as you inspect the remaining contents.

5. Repeat steps 3 and 4 until you have gone through everything that remains in the pan. Does anything look like gold?

KEY WORDS

biomes: areas where specific animals and plants live

borax: a white mineral used to make glass

erosion: the wearing away of rock or soil by water, ice, or wind

evaporation: the process by which liquid is transformed into a gas

geologists: scientists who study the structure of Earth

Great Depression: a time of economic hardship in the 1930s

heatstroke: a dangerous health condition caused by excessive heat

Ice Age: a time when glaciers covered large areas of the planet

invasive: something that intrudes or spreads itself in a harmful manner

magma: liquid rock found below Earth's surface

Mesozoic Era: a period that took place 251 to 66 million years ago

microscopic: so small that it cannot be seen with the eye alone

Paleozoic Era: a period that took place 542 to 251 million years ago

precipitation: water that falls from the sky as rain, snow, sleet, or hail

prospectors: people who search for minerals found in the ground

salt pans: flat expanses of ground covered with salt

species: groups of living things that share common traits

vision quest: a process that helps young Native Americans find purpose in life

INDEX

AV2

Get the best of both worlds.

AV2 bridges the gap between print and digital.

The expandable resources toolbar enables quick access to content including **videos**, **audio**, **activities**, **weblinks**, **slideshows**, **quizzes**, and **key words**.

Animated videos make static images come alive.

Resource icons on each page help readers to further **explore key concepts**.

Published by AV2
350 5th Avenue, 59th Floor
New York, NY 10118
Website: www.av2books.com

Library of Congress Cataloging-in-Publication Data
Names: Gagne, Tammy, author.
Title: Death Valley / Tammy Gagne and Heather Kissock.
Description: New York, NY : AV2 2021. | Series: National parks | Includes index. | Audience: Grades 4 to 6.
Identifiers: LCCN 2019009591 (print) | LCCN 2019010872 (ebook) | ISBN 9781791110680 (Multi User Ebook) | ISBN 9781791110697 (Single User Ebook) | ISBN 9781791110666 (hardcover : alk. paper) | ISBN 9781791110673 (softcover : alk. paper)
Subjects: LCSH: Death Valley National Park (Calif. and Nev.)--Juvenile literature.
Classification: LCC F868.D2 (ebook) | LCC F868.D2 G34 2019 (print) | DDC 979.4/87--dc23
LC record available at https://lccn.loc.gov/2019009591

Printed in Guangzhou, China
1 2 3 4 5 6 7 8 9 0 24 23 22 21 20

012020
101319

Project Coordinator Heather Kissock
Designers Tammy West, Ana Maria Vidal, and Terry Paulhus
Captions Heather Kissock

Photo Credits
Every reasonable effort has been made to trace ownership and to obtain permission to reprint copyright material. The publishers would be pleased to have any errors or omissions brought to their attention so that they may be corrected in subsequent printings. AV2 acknowledges Getty Images, Alamy, Minden Pictures, Newscom, iStock, and Shutterstock as its primary photo suppliers for this title.